DATE DUE

18c85

HISPANIC BIOGRAPHIES

GLORIA ESTEFAN

Singer and Entertainer

Doreen Gonzales

Enslow Publishers, Inc.

40 Industrial Road	PO Box 38
Box 398	Aldershot
Berkeley Heights, NJ 07922	Hants GU12 6BP
USA	UK

http://www.enslow.com

Dedicated to Todd and Derek.

Library of Congress Cataloging-in-Publication Data

Gonzales, Doreen.
    Gloria Estefan: singer and entertainer / Doreen Gonzales.
        p. cm. — (Hispanic biographies)
    Includes discography (p. 115), bibliographical references (p. 119), and
index.
    Summary: Presents a biography of the Cuban-born singer and
composer who has recorded such hits as "Into the Light," "Conga,"
and "Reach."
    ISBN 0-89490-890-1
    1. Estefan, Gloria—Juvenile literature. 2. Singers—United States—
Biography—Juvenile literature. [1. Estefan, Gloria. 2. Singers.
3. Cuban Americans—Biography. 4. Women—Biography.] I. Title.
II. Series.
ML3930. E85G65   1998
782. 42164'—dc21
[B]   97-42787
                                                 CIP
                                             AC MN

Illustration Credits: Eddy Rios, pp. 4, 31, 36, 92, 96, 107; Raul
DeMolina/SHOOTING STAR, pp. 7, 44, 80, 104; Created by Enslow
Publishers, Inc., p. 13; Historical Museum of Southern Florida, pp. 17,
20, 22; Brian Smith/SHOOTING STAR, pp. 48, 58; TJ Collection/
SHOOTING STAR, p. 69; Dina Alfano/SHOOTING STAR, p. 98;
Ron Davis/SHOOTING STAR, p. 108.

Cover Illustration: AP/Wide World Photos

CONTENTS

Gloria Estefan

LIKE AN ANGEL
GONE AWOL

When the lights dimmed, the crowd grew quiet. Suddenly, a keyboard broke the silence with an insistent beat. Spotlights crisscrossed the stage to reveal a curtain of multicolored ribbons. Five dancers dressed in glittering blue jumpsuits and matching headpieces leaped through the ribbons. They swooped and twirled about the stage to a melody that had now joined the keyboard's rhythm.

One dancer threw off his headpiece and shook loose his hair. A second dancer did the same, and was closely followed by two more dancers. When the last dancer unmasked, the crowd erupted in a thunderous frenzy. This was the woman the fans had come to see—this was Gloria Estefan!

The dancers lifted Estefan onto their shoulders, and she stretched her arms high in victory. It had been a year since Estefan's last concert—a year since she had been severely injured in a traffic accident. At the time, doctors were not certain that she would ever walk again. Yet in just twelve months, the singer was spinning and hopping across a stage as if she had never been hurt.

Estefan's amazing recovery had required months of painful therapy and grueling workouts. But she never quit. This determination inspired even deeper admiration from thousands of fans who were already devoted to the singer. For them, Estefan's comeback concert was just one more example of her indomitable spirit.

When the ovation subsided, Estefan launched into a medley of her old hits. The audience sang and danced along with her. Two huge screens on either side of the stage showed close-ups of the five-foot-two-inch star. She looked as fit and lovely as ever. Her signature auburn curls bounced in time to the music, and her eyes sparkled in fun. A dark beauty mark on her right cheek accentuated her perfect almond-colored complexion. But most engaging of all was Estefan's smile. It seemed to reflect the absolute joy she found in singing.

Gloria Estefan is known around the world as an exciting singer and performer. Here, a triumphant Estefan delights fans in her 1991 comeback tour, "Into the Light."

Estefan's music had evolved over several years and had been influenced by her unusual background. She had been born in Cuba but raised in Miami, Florida. While growing up in the 1960s, Estefan listened to two kinds of music: her parents' traditional Cuban music and her own generation's rock and roll.

As a teenager, Estefan joined a local band called the Miami Sound Machine. Like Estefan, the musicians were from Cuba and sang Cuban songs as well as the current pop tunes. After becoming local celebrities, the band went on a tour of Central and South America singing rock-and-roll songs in Spanish. The tour was a huge success, and the band members became instant stars. Back in the United States, however, the Miami Sound Machine remained relatively unknown.

Then the group wrote a rock-and-roll tune intended for a U.S. audience. It was sung in English, but the maracas, conga drums, and brass instruments playing in the background gave it a Cuban sound. To the band's delight, U.S. audiences loved the song. Now the Miami Sound Machine was on its way to U.S. stardom. In time, Estefan emerged as the band's lead singer, and her own popularity soared.

Today, Estefan is an international superstar. Her music has won a multitude of awards, and her recordings have sold more than one hundred million copies. She has fans all over the world who follow her career and her life.

Her fans see Estefan as more than a singer. To them, she is a caring and down-to-earth woman unspoiled by fame and fortune. They admire her integrity, her perseverance, her "girl-next-door" simplicity. She has been married to the same man since 1978, and they have a close relationship with their two children. Estefan doesn't drink, smoke, or do drugs, and she frequently participates in goodwill projects. Even the media refer to Estefan as the most positive role model in music.[1]

Although a large part of Estefan's success stems from this image, it is not what made her a superstar. Estefan's road to fame was paved by musical talent. She is an extraordinary songwriter and an exciting performer. But most impressive of all is Estefan's voice. She can croon a gentle love song or blast out the lyrics to a rock-and-roll number. No matter what she sings, Estefan's voice is impressive and memorable. It is rich and clear and full of emotion. As one writer put it, Gloria Estefan sings "like an angel gone AWOL."[2]

I'll Take Care
of You

 Gloria Estefan was born in Cuba, the largest
island in the Caribbean Sea. One hundred
thousand people were living there when Christopher
Columbus first sailed to its shores in 1492. In 1511,
Spaniards came searching for gold. The Spaniards then
turned to raising sugarcane and enslaved indigenous
(native) Cubans. These Cubans were forced to work so
hard that many died from exhaustion. Thousands
more died from Old World diseases they had never
been exposed to before. By the mid-1500s, Cuba's

indigenous population had fallen from one hundred thousand to less than three thousand.[1] So the Spaniards enslaved Africans to work on their farms.

Gradually, Cuban society developed into four classes. The most elite class was made up of people from Spain. They were wealthy, held important government jobs, and made the laws. Then came the Creoles—people of Spanish descent who had been born in Cuba. Next were people of mixed Spanish, African, or indigenous ancestry. People of pure African heritage were at the bottom of Cuba's social system. They were poor and uneducated. Discriminatory laws kept them from pursuing an education or any professional opportunities.

In 1895, a Cuban named José Martí led a rebellion against Spanish rule. Martí also sought economic independence from the United States and its citizens who had business interests in Cuba worth more than $50 million.[2] When Martí's rebellion spread, the U.S. government sent a battleship to the island to protect its people and its property. In February 1898, an explosion on the ship killed 260 soldiers. The United States blamed Spain for the incident, declared war, and began helping the Cuban rebels. By the end of the year, Spain had surrendered Cuba.

Cubans struggled to create a democracy for the next fifty years. But leaders came to power through force and seemed more interested in becoming wealthy than in building a democratic nation. One

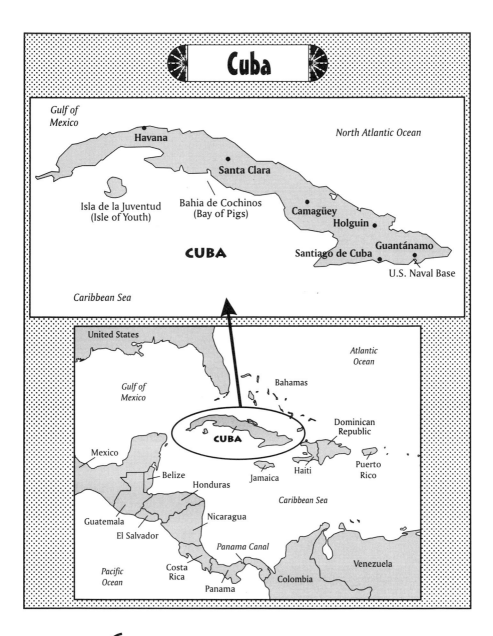

Cuba is the largest island in the Caribbean Sea.

such leader, Fulgencio Batista, ruled almost without interruption from 1933 to 1959. Batista's policies helped a few Cubans get rich while most Cubans remained poor.

Gloria Estefan's parents grew up during Batista's rule. Her father, José Manuel Fajardo, was a strong, athletic young man. He joined the Cuban army and became a bodyguard for President Batista's family. Fajardo's wife, Gloria, was a well-educated teacher and a talented singer. Between their two incomes, the Fajardos lived comfortably in Havana, Cuba's capital and largest city.[3]

Many Cubans, however, were still poor. Some formed secret armies to revolt against Batista. The most powerful revolutionary group was led by a young lawyer named Fidel Castro. Castro organized several successful attacks on Batista's soldiers, but each victory brought a retaliatory move from Batista. He canceled elections, banned free speech, censored the press, and threw people who opposed him into prison. He even executed rebels, and it is believed that Batista ordered the killing of more than twenty thousand Cubans. With each act of brutality, more Cubans turned against Batista.

As Castro's forces waged war on Batista's government, José and Gloria Fajardo started a family. Their first child was born on September 1, 1957. The Fajardos named their daughter Gloria Marie after her mother. They called her Glorita, meaning "little Gloria." As Glorita approached her first birthday, Fidel Castro and his rebels gained support throughout Cuba.

By December 1958, Castro prepared to take over Cuba and rid the government of Batista supporters. Castro sent some of them out of Cuba. He had others executed. Many, like Gloria's father, were thrown into jail. Gloria's mother once took her to the prison to visit him. Though she was still very young, Gloria would remember this visit into her adulthood.[4]

Staying in Cuba was now dangerous for anyone who had been connected with Batista's government. So the Fajardos made plans to leave the island as soon as possible. When Gloria's father was released from prison, the family bought three round-trip tickets to the United States, not wanting to raise suspicions that they were fleeing Cuba. But officials at Havana's airport still checked them carefully to see that they were not taking much with them. They even tore up Mrs. Fajardo's college diploma. Consequently, the Fajardos left Cuba with the clothing on their backs, a couple of suitcases, and return tickets to Cuba. Not one of the tickets was ever used. Gloria, in fact, still has hers.

Gloria arrived in the United States in December 1958, when she was sixteen months old. For a while, the Fajardos used newspapers for bedsheets and food cans for cookware. By the autumn of 1959, the family had settled into a tiny apartment behind the Orange

Bowl Stadium in Miami, Florida. Other exiles from Batista's government lived nearby.

These Cubans watched from afar as Castro turned Cuba into a communist country. In a communist nation, the government owns everything in an attempt to divide the country's wealth equally. The government decides how much money each citizen should make and pays everyone's wages.

Many Cubans supported Castro and his communist government. They believed it would lift them from poverty. But others opposed communism because they did not want their lives to be controlled by the government. In general, the anticommunists were wealthy or middle-class citizens with college educations. Thousands of them left the island for Spain or South or Central America. The majority, however, moved to Miami, Florida, believing that Castro's rule would be short. They planned to return to Cuba just as soon as he was thrown from power.

By 1961, 135,000 Cubans had moved to Miami, increasing the city's population by one third. Cuban men took whatever jobs they could find, and some Cuban women worked, too. They lived in the same neighborhood as the Fajardos, and everyone spoke Spanish, celebrated Cuban holidays, listened to Cuban music, and ate Cuban food. The community seemed so much like Cuba, in fact, it became known as "Little Havana."

This photograph of Havana, Cuba, was taken soon after Gloria Estefan's parents immigrated to the United States.

This huge influx of Cuban immigrants was so difficult for some Miami residents to accept that they discriminated against the refugees.[5] For example, several apartment buildings posted signs saying, "No children, no pets, no Cubans." As an adult, Estefan remembered how much this prejudice upset her mother.[6]

While many Cubans in Miami dreamed of returning to Cuba, Castro made friends with another communist country, the Soviet Union. The Soviet Union and the United States were then engaged in what was known as the Cold War. There were no military battles in the Cold War. Instead, the two countries fought each other with words and secret maneuvers, each afraid that the other might try to take it over by using nuclear weapons.

Consequently, the friendship between Cuba and the Soviet Union worried the United States. If Cuba formed an alliance with the Soviets, the Soviets might establish a military base on Cuba. This would pose a serious threat to United States security since Cuba was so close. Soon the Central Intelligence Agency (CIA) became involved. The CIA is the government agency that watches foreign countries to keep the United States safe.

CIA officials decided that Fidel Castro must be overthrown to keep the Soviets out of Cuba. The agency recruited fourteen hundred Cubans for a secret mission to oust Castro. José Fajardo was one. The men would land on Cuba at the Bay of Pigs. Then they would march to Havana and capture Castro. The CIA promised to protect the force with cover from the air. In addition, the agency believed that thousands of unhappy Cubans would join the refugees in their fight.

On April 17, 1961, Fajardo led the force's tank division onto the island. But Castro's army was ready and waiting and pinned down the troops in hours. United States air cover never came. Neither did aid from people living on the island. In fact, many Cubans rallied to Castro's defense. Four days after the refugees landed at the Bay of Pigs, Cuba had captured and jailed more than a thousand men, including Fajardo.

Gloria's mother kept the bad news from Gloria. The three-year-old could not possibly understand the political events surrounding her father's imprisonment, anyway. Of course, Gloria did know that her father was gone. But whenever she asked where he was, her mother would say that he was "on the farm."

Days turned into weeks and weeks into months, and Gloria's father still did not come home. Whenever she asked about him, her mother stuck to her original story. But Gloria was not fooled. Maybe she remembered that the last time her father had been gone he had been in jail. Or maybe she overheard people talking about him. But somehow Gloria deduced that her father was in prison. Yet her main concern was for her

Fidel Castro (left) talks with then-vice president of the United States, Richard M. Nixon.

mother's feelings. She once told some guests, "Don't tell my mom my dad's in prison. She thinks he's a farmer."[7]

In the meantime, Gloria's mother filled their home with music. She had a large collection of Cuban records that she played and sang along with. Gloria sang, too, learning traditional and contemporary Cuban songs.

Then came the Christmas of 1962, and the Fajardo family received a special gift. United States President John F. Kennedy had persuaded Castro to release the Bay of Pigs prisoners in exchange for $53 million in the form of food and medicine. At last, Gloria's father was home.

Fajardo's ordeal had not extinguished his dreams. He still hoped that his homeland could be freed from communism. Fajardo believed that if he did something to help the U.S. government, it would keep trying to free Cuba.[8] So Gloria's father enlisted in the U.S. Army. In 1963, he was assigned to Lackland Air Force Base near San Antonio, Texas, and the Fajardos moved to Texas.

Gloria started first grade in Texas. She soon discovered that she was the only pupil in her class who could not speak English. She met this challenge with enthusiasm and in six months was reading English so well that she won an award.

President John F. Kennedy (bottom, right) welcomes home soldiers who had been captured at the Bay of Pigs.

Another language was gripping the young girl: the language of music. The adult Gloria once explained how music had been so important in her childhood that "specific events, sights and even smells are forever linked to the songs that I heard playing at that time."[9] This is what happened the day she went to a laundromat with her mother and a popular song, "Ferry Across the Mersey," came on the car's radio. The song was a soft rock-and-roll melody with an eerie, haunting quality. "It gave me goosebumps," Estefan later recalled, "and I refused to get out of the car. . . . I didn't know what a ferry was, let alone the Mersey, but there was such longing in that song, it really reached me. Whenever I hear that song, I can still smell the laundromat."[10]

While living in Texas, the Fajardos had a second child, whom they named Rebecca. Then another political conflict entered their lives. Two forces in an Asian country called Vietnam were battling for control of the government. One group wanted communist rule, the other wanted democracy. The United States joined the fight, supporting the forces of democracy. In 1966, Gloria's father was sent to Vietnam. Gloria, Rebecca, and their mother stayed behind.

Gloria celebrated her ninth birthday that September. Her present was a guitar that her mother had asked a friend to bring back from Spain. Gloria was thrilled with the gift.[11] But she hated the music lessons her mother made her take. They seemed slow and tedious, and Gloria felt they took the fun out of playing.[12] She stuck with them, though, while also learning to pluck out tunes on her own.

When Gloria's father returned from Vietnam in 1968, the family moved back to Miami. It was the place they now considered home. But the happy homecoming turned sour when Gloria's father began showing signs of illness. He would fall down for no reason or stop at streetlights when they were green. Doctors decided Fajardo had multiple sclerosis.[13] Multiple sclerosis (MS) is a disease that destroys the nervous system, making a person weak and unable to control his muscles. Soon Gloria's father was bedridden and needed someone to take care of him.

This left the Fajardos without an income. Although Gloria's mother was a trained and experienced teacher, she could not teach without the credentials the Cuban officials had torn up at Havana's airport. So she found a different job and went to college at night to earn a teaching certificate. While her mother was away, Gloria took care of her father, her sister, and the house. The strain of this huge responsibility often showed on the young girl's face. Gloria remembers, "I looked so much older than I do now because I was carrying the weight of the whole world on my shoulders."[14]

When Gloria's mother received her teaching degree, she found a job at a Miami school. This helped the family financially, but she was still gone much of the time. So Gloria continued to come home from school every day to care for her father and her sister. At times she wished she could hang out with friends or join school clubs. But she never complained because she did not want to let her family down.[15] Added to the burden of her duties was the sorrow she felt for her father whose health kept growing worse.[16]

So Gloria created a refuge for herself. When she finished her chores each day, she retreated to her bedroom and locked the door. Then she picked up her guitar and sang. Gloria sang the Cuban songs her mother had taught to her. She sang the tunes she heard on the radio. She sang songs from songbooks she checked out of the library. "Music," Gloria later reported, "was the one bright spot in my life."[17] Indeed, the young girl sang with all her might, trying to soothe her heartaches with song.

CHAPTER THREE

WHAT A DIFFERENCE A DAY MAKES

Gloria started junior high at a Catholic school for girls called Our Lady of Lourdes. She was an attractive young woman with glowing eyes and dark, wavy hair. But like so many other teens, she was sensitive about her looks, and particularly about her weight. The adult Gloria once said, "When I was a teenager, I was fat. I was shy, I wore glasses, I had one big eyebrow and hair all over my body."[1] During her teen years, Gloria did not go to many parties or have any dates.

Yet Gloria's poor social life may have been due to her responsibilities at home more than her looks. By the time she was sixteen, Mr. Fajardo's health had deteriorated drastically. Because he needed constant care, Mrs. Fajardo placed him in a Miami veteran's hospital. There nurses could take care of him twenty-four hours a day. Even so, Gloria visited her father often. She continued to help out at home as well.

Gloria still made time for music. Among her favorite musicians were Barbra Streisand, Diana Ross, and Karen Carpenter.[2] Gloria also liked a singer named Carole King. She owned one of King's most famous albums, a collection of soft-rock songs with thought-provoking lyrics. "I probably wore out my copy of [Carole King's *Tapestry* album]," Gloria later said, "I know I wore out my mother listening to it! It's one of the must influential albums, as a total album, in my life."[3]

Although she was still shy, music sometimes pulled Gloria out of her shell. She played her guitar and sang in school talent shows. She also performed for her friends. One song they liked hearing was "Don't Let the Sun Catch You Crying," a tune by Jerry and the Pacemakers, the same band that had sung "Ferry Across the Mersey." Gloria often teamed up with her cousin Merci to play and sing. For Gloria, these singing sessions were sheer fun. Merci, however, took them more seriously because she wanted to be in show business.

When she was not singing, Gloria was a quiet young lady. Her interest in words and language had grown into a passion for writing poetry. She worked hard at school, learning what would be her third language: French. Actually, Gloria was a conscientious student in all her classes. She was so serious, in fact, that several of the nuns at Lourdes predicted she would become a nun herself.

Gloria had different plans. In 1975, she graduated from Our Lady of Lourdes Academy with straight As, a partial scholarship to the University of Miami, and dreams of becoming a teacher. That spring, Gloria and a few friends began practicing for a performance they were giving at a relative's birthday party. At one rehearsal, the girls met a man named Emilio Estefan. Emilio was in a local band and had been asked to help the girls with their upcoming show. As shy as ever, Gloria said little to Emilio during their first meeting.

Gloria started college in the autumn. When she was not attending classes, she worked at a Miami airport translating Spanish into English for travelers. She enjoyed this job so much that she considered making language interpretation her career. Then she took a class in psychology and changed her goals again. Now she decided to become a psychologist.

That autumn Gloria and her mother went to a wedding. Coincidentally, Emilio Estefan's band, the Miami Latin Boys, was playing at the reception. During one of the band's breaks, Emilio noticed Gloria and remembered the young lady he had met a few months earlier. He asked her to sing a couple of songs with his band. At first Gloria refused. But prodding from Emilio and Mrs. Fajardo finally coaxed her onto the stage. The other musicians were not very happy to see her, though. They worried that an amateur singer would embarrass the band.[4] Gloria must have surprised them all. She sang so beautifully that night, she received a standing ovation from the crowd.

Apparently, the wedding guests were not the only ones who recognized Gloria's talent. The Miami Latin Boys faced stiff competition from other local bands, and Emilio was always looking for ways to make his ensemble unique. Because the other bands were all-male, a female would make Emilio's band special. Of course, not just any female would help. But the warmth and sincerity in Gloria's voice impressed Emilio. A couple of days after the wedding, he called her and asked her to join the band.

Gloria said no. She was too busy with college and could not be distracted from her studies. But Emilio did not give up. In a few weeks, he called her back. This time he promised that the job would not interfere with her classes. He told her that she would have to work only on weekends and during vacations.

Now Gloria accepted Emilio's offer, thinking it would be a fun way to earn money. There was only most of her time at the rear, playing maracas and singing backup. The other band members took turns singing the lead parts. They were Juan Marcos Avila who played the guitar, drummer Enrique "Kiki" Garcia, Raul Murciano on the saxophone, and Emilio Estefan, who played keyboards and percussion. They all worked together well and liked one another, especially Murciano and Merci Fajardo. They began dating and eventually married.

Joining the band changed Gloria's life, too. "All of a sudden I was going to parties every weekend," she said, "singing with a whole band behind me, making money for it, and enjoying every second."[6] She also liked being around Emilio, and she was soon feeling more than just professional admiration for the man. But Gloria never let on that she was attracted to Emilio. He was five years older than she was, and he dated women in their thirties. Gloria did not think Emilio could possibly be interested in an unsophisticated eighteen-year-old like herself.[7]

Furthermore, Gloria did not want a failed romance to ruin her job.[8] She still planned to become a psychologist, and singing with the band was helping her reach that goal. She was not about to jeopardize the job that was paying for her education.

Actually, Emilio had found Gloria beautiful the moment he met her.[9] But he knew she had experienced a difficult childhood, and he did not want her to be hurt anymore. Therefore, he decided to wait until he was seriously interested in her before asking her out. So the two musicians worked side by side for several months without ever knowing of their mutual attraction. During this time, Gloria got to know Estefan better.

Emilio Estefan was born in Lebanon. His parents moved to Cuba when he was young. Although no one in his family was a musician, little Emilio was particularly fond of music. He taught himself to play the accordion when he was six years old. The Estefans stayed in Cuba when Castro rose to power, hoping they could keep the factory they owned. But by 1965 it was clear that the government would take control of it, just as it was taking over all other businesses. So thirteen-year-old Emilio and his father left Cuba. José, Emilio's older brother, could not go with them. Castro's laws required him to stay in Cuba because he was of draft age. So he and Emilio's mother stayed behind, hoping that one day they, too, could leave.

Emilio and his father went to Spain first. Then, they moved to Miami, where they lived with fifteen other relatives. Although Emilio did not speak English, he quickly found ways to make money. After school he worked at various odd jobs: running errands for elderly women, selling T-shirts, even staging beauty contests in the neighborhood.

In 1966, Emilio became a mail clerk for Bacardi Imports. Bacardi made rum from the sugarcane grown on various Caribbean islands. Emilio was an enthusiastic and industrious employee, and he was promoted from one job to the next. In only twelve years he worked his way up to being the head of the company's Latin American marketing department. Latin America is a name that refers to Mexico and the countries of Central and South America.

Emilio Estefan now had an important and well-paying job. Yet his real passion was music. In the evenings and on weekends, he played his accordion at a restaurant for tips. When Estefan's boss at Bacardi heard he was a musician, he hired him to entertain at a party. Estefan took along two other musicians, and their first gig was a success. This job led to other engagements, and Estefan kept adding musicians to his band. By 1974, the band had several members, a name, and a private rehearsing studio—the one-car garage at Estefan's aunt's house.

The Miami Latin Boys played a variety of music, carefully choosing the songs they would play for each performance, according to the audience. In general, younger crowds liked rock music and older audiences liked softer music. Sometimes the band sang in English and other times in Spanish. When the audience was Cuban, the Miami Latin Boys played the music of their homeland.

Cuban music is a unique blend of Spanish and African sounds. Traditional Spanish music depends

Even after achieving international fame, Gloria and Emilio Estefan performed often in their hometown of Miami, Florida.

heavily on guitars. African music is dominated by drums. As the two groups on the island merged, their music mixed, too, giving birth to new sounds and rhythms. Some of the rhythms had their own names.

For example, there was the conga. The conga rhythm was named for the drum on which it was played. The first conga drums were made from hollowed tree trunks covered with animal hides. Modern conga drums are long cylinders manufactured from wood. They are held between the knees and played with the fingers and the hands. Many Cuban songs use conga drums for percussion. A song with a heavy fourth beat is known specifically as a conga.

Congas are lively tunes meant to inspire people to dance. Conga dancers form a long line and wind through a dance hall, stepping in time to the music. On every fourth beat of the drum, the dancers pause to kick out a foot. Traditionally, a conga is the last song of the night.

In addition to congas, the Miami Latin Boys played the distinctive rhythms of other Latin American countries. They also performed the music of various ethnic groups in the United States. Band member Avila once pointed out, "Our sound evolved from trying to please all the people. Here in Miami, we have Cubans, Anglos, blacks, South Americans. You have to be very versatile."[10] They were. Between their willingness to work hard and their musical talent, the Miami Latin

Boys built a steady business. At times they entertained at three different parties in one night.

When Gloria first started singing with Estefan's band, she was not familiar with some of the Latin American music the group performed. So she listened to records by famous Latin American singers to educate herself. One of her favorites was a woman named Celia Cruz.[11] In this way, being a member of the MSM expanded Gloria's musical repertoire. Gloria expanded the repertoire of the band, too. She added ballads. Ballads are songs that tell stories or explain feelings. They are sung more slowly than dance tunes, and they rely on words and melodies rather than on rhythms.

As the months passed, Estefan watched Gloria with growing affection. On the two hundredth birthday of the United States, he decided to tell her how he felt. That night, the MSM was playing at a party aboard a ship. During one of the band's breaks, the two walked up on deck to look at the stars. Emilio told Gloria it was his birthday, too. He was only teasing, but Gloria gave him a "birthday" kiss anyway. The two went on their first date that very night, and it was the start of something big.

Now Gloria studied, rehearsed, performed, and developed a romance. Then she added another project to her impossibly full schedule. She began to exercise and diet to reshape her body. As her efforts began to pay off, Emilio made what seemed to be a terribly insensitive remark. He told Gloria that she could improve herself by 95 percent. Angrily, she replied, "If you think I could improve myself ninety-five percent, then why are you bothering with me now? You only like five percent of me? What if I don't improve? What if I don't change?"[12]

However, Gloria continued dating Emilio. In time she realized that his comment had actually been a compliment. Emilio saw a tremendous untapped potential in Gloria, and he was encouraging her to develop it. It would not be long before the rest of the world would see what he meant.

CHAPTER FOUR

BORN TO SING

 During 1978, Gloria's life seemed to be on fast forward. First, she graduated from college with a degree in psychology and communications. Although Gloria never became a practicing psychologist, she was always glad she had finished college. She believed her education helped her understand herself better.[1]

After college, Gloria joined the Miami Sound Machine full time. Then came what may have been the most significant event in Gloria's adult life: She married Emilio Estefan. The two had a small wedding on

September 1, Gloria's birthday, and went to Japan for their honeymoon.

That same year, Emilio Estefan's older brother José decided to leave Cuba with his family. But by now Castro's government made it very difficult to get off the island. So when the authorities learned of José Estefan's plan, his family had to go into hiding for two months. Fortunately, Gloria was able to visit the island during this time and secretly supplied the family with food. This was Gloria Estefan's first trip to Cuba since fleeing in 1959. The country saddened her. The communist government's control of everything made her feel claustrophobic.[2] During the visit, Gloria promised herself never to perform in Cuba while Castro was in power.

That same year, the MSM took a giant step in its musical career when it released its first album. The record included Cuban songs, popular U.S. tunes, and ballads. It was produced by a Miami company, with the songs sung in English on one side and in Spanish on the other. This recording enjoyed enough local success for the MSM to produce two more albums. These were also "cut" in both Spanish and English. Songs from the three recordings were regularly broadcast on the Miami radio stations that played Latin American music.

Gloria Estefan's father died in 1980, bringing sorrow into her life. But the year also brought joy when

Gloria had her first baby. The Estefans named him Nayib, and Gloria said her son was the most important thing in her life. She did not stop her singing career to become a full-time mother, though. "I don't feel that you're supposed to give up your career for your children," she said. "When you give up something of yourself, you're usually not as happy as you were before. And if you're not happy with yourself, it's very hard to make someone else happy."[3]

Consequently, the Estefans took Nayib with them to rehearsals, recording sessions, and even performances. When it was impossible for either of them to care for Nayib, he stayed with Gloria's mother or sister or with one of Emilio's relatives.

The MSM was now as successful as it could be in Miami. The members were ready to move into the national arena. To do so, the group needed a recording contract from a major music company. So Emilio Estefan quit his $100,000-a-year job with Bacardi to devote all of his time to finding a record company interested in his band.

Recording and selling popular music is a billion-dollar industry in the United States. Popular ("pop") music includes jazz, rock, country western, and songs written for stage shows and movies. Thousands of pop songs are recorded in the United States annually and sold all over the world. This requires advertising.

Gloria began a regular workout program in the 1980s, and she continues it today. Here she runs with her personal trainer, Basilio Mercado.

One common advertising method is through airplay. Each time a radio station plays a song, that song is being advertised. Therefore, recording companies use distributors to sell their songs to the radio stations that will most likely play them. Jazz songs are sent to stations that play jazz music and are said to have a jazz format. Rock songs are sent to stations with a rock format, and so on. Record companies pay close attention to which songs get played on the air. They also keep a careful watch on which songs people buy.

The people who buy music are known as the *music market*. This market is divided into categories, according to music type. For instance, the people who buy country music make up the country music market. Several music magazines monitor the various markets. One of the most well known of these is *Billboard* magazine. Every week *Billboard* ranks songs within each market, according to how many recordings of that song were purchased. These ranked lists are called charts. Record companies study the charts to learn which songs people are buying. This helps the companies predict what recordings will sell well.

In 1980, Emilio Estefan approached a major record company called CBS Records. After listening to the MSM's latest music, CBS executives may have felt as if they had struck gold. CBS knew that United States-style rock and roll was becoming popular in Latin America. The company believed that the music would be even more appealing if Latin Americans could sing along with it in their own language.[4] For the majority, this would be Spanish. When Emilio knocked at CBS's door, he put his band in the right place at the right time.

CBS promptly offered the MSM a contract to record pop tunes in Spanish. Though the band members really wanted to break into the U.S. pop market, they saw CBS's offer as a great opportunity.[5] If the MSM was successful in Latin America, it could try to make it in the United States later. So the band members signed a recording contract with Discos CBS International, a division of the company that was based in Miami.

In 1981, the MSM recorded its first all-Spanish album. It included original pop tunes, dance numbers, and ballads sung in Spanish. Everyone in the band helped write the songs for the record, but Kiki was especially productive. Tunes flowed from him nonstop, and he penned catchy lyrics for each. He wrote these words in English, then gave them to Gloria to translate into Spanish. Gloria wrote songs, too. She created the ballads that MSM sang. Emilio acted as the band's boss, making all final decisions regarding business matters.

Soon after this first album was released, the MSM went on a concert tour throughout Latin America. The combination of Spanish lyrics, American rock and roll, and live performances spawned a success the MSM had only dreamed of. Everywhere the band went, its songs were being played on local radio stations. When one song began to lose popularity, another one took its place. As song after song became a hit, magazine and newspaper reporters scrambled to write about the newest celebrities of Latin American pop.

While his parents found fame, Nayib stayed with relatives in Miami. Because Gloria missed him terribly, she kept herself busy by working on her act. Losing weight had increased her self-confidence, and now she started adding simple dance steps to her performances. This brought her to center stage more often, a place that was still scary for her.[6] So she studied videotapes of MSM concerts to improve her part of the performance. But this was such a painful experience for Gloria that she often watched the tapes with her hands over her eyes, peeking out between her fingers.[7]

Then in 1982, Gloria Estefan stepped onto a stage in Chile all by herself. As she looked out at sixty thousand expectant faces, her knees literally began to knock in fear. "It was one of the most difficult experiences of my life," she reported.[8] If it was Gloria's willpower that started this solo, it was her talent that finished it, for the song received a booming ovation. This success led to more solos, and by the end of the year, Gloria had become the band's lead singer.

Of course, this did not mean that Gloria quit trying to make her act better. "I'm a perfectionist," she later

The Miami Sound Machine first became famous in Latin American countries, where Gloria and the band performed pop songs in Spanish.

told a writer, "and once I was [in the spotlight] it was do it right or get out."[9]

In the meantime, Emilio made concert arrangements, collected the band's pay, and paid the MSM musicians. Some of the musicians did not like Emilio's taking charge of the band's finances, but no one told him so—except Murciano.[10] One day in 1982 Murciano asked Emilio for a raise. Unfortunately, their conversation turned into an argument and Murciano quit the band.[11] His wife, Merci, left too.

Even without the couple, though, the MSM had become one of the most popular bands in the Spanish-speaking world. By the end of 1983, the musicians had produced four albums that had sold millions of copies from Mexico to Argentina and Peru to Brazil. Furthermore, concerts regularly filled soccer stadiums with thirty thousand to forty thousand people.

Yet for all its fame in Latin America, few people in the United States had ever heard of the Miami Sound Machine. When the band appeared in the States, only three to four thousand people came to see the show.

Now Gloria Estefan had a new goal.

BREAKTHROUGH!

In 1984, Kiki Garcia wrote a song called "Dr. Beat." As usual, he gave the lyrics to Gloria to translate into Spanish. But Gloria could not get the Spanish words to go with the song's music. Emilio saw her problem as an opportunity. Perhaps, he thought, "Dr. Beat" was meant to be sung in English. Maybe it was the song that would break the Miami Sound Machine into the U.S. pop market. Emilio took his idea to CBS Records.

CBS promptly rejected it. Company executives were not eager to change anything the MSM was doing.[1] The band was hugely successful in Latin America. To try to move into another market might be disastrous. Indeed, several other musicians had attempted the move before and most had failed.

There were, however, occasional success stories. In fact, just as Emilio Estefan was discussing his proposal with CBS, one Spanish singer was making his way into the U.S. pop market. Julio Iglesias had been famous throughout the Spanish-speaking world for many years. Now he was recording songs in English and his music was gaining wide appeal in the United States. Increasingly, Iglesias could be heard on radio stations with a Latin format, as well as on those with a U.S. pop format. When a song is popular in more than one format, it is said to have crossed over from one market into another. Such a song is dubbed a "crossover," and its musician is called a "crossover musician."

Record companies like crossover musicians because their music is purchased by people from two different markets. Obviously, this increases a company's profits. But successful, consistent crossover artists are rare. CBS knew that only a few people had ever before crossed from the Latin market to the U.S. pop market. Based on this, the company told Emilio that his crossover dreams were a bad idea.

But Emilio was not discouraged. Gloria, too, was determined. She believed the MSM had advantages other Latin artists did not have.[2] For instance, the band members had all grown up in the United States listening to pop music. They were fluent in English, and they had performed in English before. So Emilio Estefan kept trying to persuade CBS to record "Dr. Beat" in English. He finally succeeded.

As expected, Miami radio stations with a Latin format played the band's newest song. More important though, "Dr. Beat" was also played on Miami stations with pop formats. Then, to everyone's delight, "Dr. Beat" found its way onto pop music stations all over the United States.

The success of "Dr. Beat" was largely due to its appeal in U.S. discotheques. Discotheques, or discos, were nightclubs where couples danced to music being played on stereos. Disco dancers relied on music with a steady rhythmic beat for performing their steps. Because "Dr. Beat" had strong percussions, the tune was perfect for disco dancing.

Then the song jumped across the Atlantic to discos in the Netherlands. Soon "Dr. Beat" was as popular there as it was in the United States. The number next traveled to England and to other European countries. By the end of 1984, "Dr. Beat" was a favorite in discos all across the United States and Europe.

Just as thrilling as the song's international success was the moment it hit *Billboard* magazine's dance chart. Although "Dr. Beat" never went higher than number ten on the dance chart, its mere appearance elated the band. More than ever, the members believed that MSM could command a following in the U.S. pop market. Now Emilio Estefan convinced CBS to produce an entire MSM album in English. To do so, CBS moved the band to Epic Records, a division of the company that handled international rock music.

The musicians went to work. There would be ten songs on the English album, including "Dr. Beat." Kiki wrote four more songs, Gloria wrote two more, and the remaining three songs were a collaboration among various group members. The album was called *Eyes of Innocence* and was released in 1984. On its cover was a photograph of the band's four members: Gloria, Emilio, Kiki, and Avila.

Disappointingly, *Eyes of Innocence* never climbed onto one album chart. But the MSM musicians were not defeated. They soon embarked on another advertising campaign. This time the band crossed the Atlantic Ocean to give concerts in the Netherlands and in England. In Amsterdam, Gloria suggested that the MSM add a conga to its show. Emilio did not like the idea at first, but she changed his mind.[3] When the MSM ended its next concert with a conga song in Spanish, the audience went wild.

The crowd's enthusiasm fired Estefan. She suggested that the band write a new song, a song with English lyrics and a conga beat. Kiki went to work immediately. By the time the MSM arrived at its next stop, he had completed the song that Gloria had envisioned. It was simply titled "Conga."

When the band played the song for the CBS executives, they did not like it. One told Gloria that the song was "too Latin for the Americans and too American for the Latins."[4] She promptly thanked him, saying that that was exactly what the band members were. Perhaps it was her confidence that persuaded CBS to produce the song. Then "Conga" was released to radio stations, and many disc jockeys also said the song sounded too foreign for U.S. audiences. Once more, though, Gloria's intuitions proved correct. "Conga" quickly became the most requested song on pop stations all across the United States. In September 1985, the song hit *Billboard*'s dance chart, and by mid-November it had worked its way up to number one.

Then the song did something truly extraordinary— it hopped onto four different *Billboard* charts at once: dance, pop, Latin, and African American. This was the first song in recording history to accomplish such a feat. Eventually, the song worked its way up the pop chart to the number-ten position. For the first time ever, the MSM had a top-ten song on the U.S. pop chart.

Gloria took little time to bask in the glory of the achievement. She and the other band members were busy making a new album called *Primitive Love*. It would include the hit song "Conga." Now, Emilio Estefan hired three new musicians. Joe Galdo, Rafael Vigil, and Lawrence Dermer called themselves the Three Jerks. The Jerks wrote several songs for *Primitive Love*, and three of them were crafted especially for Gloria Estefan's voice range and qualities.

Another song slated for the album was a ballad Gloria had written after arguing with Emilio. Realizing that she had not expressed herself very well, Gloria retreated to her room, where she picked up her guitar. Now words streamed forth. Before long, Gloria had composed a new song entitled "Words Get in the Way."

In 1986, *Primitive Love* was released. On its cover was a photo of Gloria. On the back were separate photos of her and three other band members—Emilio, Kiki, and Avila. There were, however, no photos of the Jerks, and according to Galdo, a person needed a "magnifying glass" to see their credits on the album's jacket.[5]

America, however, did not seem to mind. Suddenly, the Miami Sound Machine was the hottest "new" band in the country. Since most people had never heard of the group before "Conga" became a hit, it was as if the MSM had appeared out of nowhere. Within weeks, two other songs from the *Primitive Love* album climbed onto the top-ten charts: "Bad Boys" and Gloria Estefan's ballad, "Words Get in the Way."

"Words Get in the Way" would later be seen as a turning point in Gloria's career. It showcased her rich, melodic voice, proving she was a talented singer who did not need complicated instrumentation behind her to sound good. Some music critics compared her voice with that of pop musician Karen Carpenter. This did not surprise Gloria, for she had spent hours in her youth singing along with Carpenter's radio hits.[6]

A U.S. concert tour soon followed the release of *Primitive Love*. These performances drew larger and larger audiences. Kiki's unharnessed enthusiasm made him a favorite of the fans, and the media called him the "spirit of Miami Sound Machine."[7] During concerts he was in constant motion playing his drums or dancing beside Gloria Estefan.

Gloria herself was no slouch. One writer called her the "hot shot of energy onstage."[8] In addition to singing, she performed simple choreographed steps and hopped across the stage in music-inspired dancing. Listeners seemed incapable of sitting still while Gloria danced and the band beat out its rhythms. "Conga" ended every MSM concert, and audience members often took the song's advice to "let the music move your feet."[9] At one performance, in Vermont, the song inspired eleven thousand people to dance in what may have been the world's longest conga line!

With fame came wealth. Gloria and Emilio Estefan pose in the mid-1980s on the hood of their new Rolls Royce.

The band's dreams of success in the United States were becoming a reality. By blending the sounds of pop with Latin American instruments, rhythms, and timing, the MSM had created something new and enticing. From coast to coast, the band entertained crowds with its spicy, Latin-flavored numbers. Eventually, *Primitive Love* sold 2 million copies. The band remained popular in other countries, too. By the end of 1985, the Miami Sound Machine was playing to eager audiences all over the world. A few of these concerts were especially memorable.

In El Salvador, for instance, the band was ushered onstage by three heavily armed bodyguards because of a bloody civil war raging there. Suddenly, loud cracks rang out and the band members flung themselves to the floor, fearing they were under attack. When nothing more happened, the musicians looked up to discover that the sounds were just fireworks being set off to greet them. Somewhat embarrassed, they climbed to their feet, brushed themselves off, and joined the laughter coming from the audience.[10]

Then the MSM represented the United States at a music fair in Tokyo. Before playing, fair officials warned the group not to be disappointed by a quiet response from the audience. They explained that the Japanese people were reserved and that even superb performances were greeted with little more than polite applause. Imagine the band's surprise when the audience jumped up during the first number and began to dance. People danced through the entire act and even came onstage to dance with the band.[11] Predictably, the MSM took home the fair's first prize.

Yet in spite of international fame, the Estefans still arranged their schedules so that there was always a parent or relative taking care of Nayib. At six years of age, he looked a lot like his father. Gloria described her son as having a dry sense of humor. He was also filled with confidence, and Gloria sometimes joked that he should have been named Napoleon. But inside, she was glad Nayib was strong. This quality, she remarked, came in handy when one's family was famous.[12]

Gloria seemed to think of the band members as family, too. In one interview she reported that they all enjoyed one another's company, onstage and off. She went on to say, "The four of us are very close. We get along fine. [When we don't] we talk out our differences in Spanish."[13]

By now, Gloria was an indispensable member of this foursome. She was a nonstop performer who excited fans. In addition, there was a touch of seductiveness in Gloria's show. She danced playfully next to the musicians in staged flirtation and wore tasteful but slightly sexy costumes. She might bare a shoulder, for example, or let a dress dip low in front. Yet there was a purity to Gloria too, and she proudly proclaimed that Emilio had been her only boyfriend.[14]

Offstage, Gloria's gift for setting poetry to music was just as vital to the band. She wrote lyrics and melodies that were praised for their natural flow. Her songs told about the joys and sorrows in her life. These seemed to be the same joys and sorrows of the fans Estefan had never met. Furthermore, her passionate voice made people feel what the singer was feeling. "My business," Gloria once commented, "is to try to evoke emotion."[15]

But Gloria didn't spend much time analyzing her songwriting. She simply wrote. Sometimes she began with a title and wrote a whole song to go with it. Other times she wrote entire songs without once thinking about a title. What never changed was her continual need to write. She filled notebooks with ideas, writing wherever and whenever she could. She wrote at home, between taping sessions, in hotel rooms, and on the band's tour bus. Perhaps most important, Gloria had the drive to "do it right." She might work on a song for months before ever letting anyone else hear it. During this time, she would sing the words to herself over and over again until they were perfect.

The MSM seemed to have found a winning formula with Gloria as a major songwriter and the lead singer. In addition to hit songs and huge concerts, the band recorded music for two movies, *Top Gun* and *Stakeout*. And at the 1986 American Music Awards, the MSM was named the "best new pop artists" and "top pop singles artists."

To the Cuban people of Miami, though, the MSM was much more than just a successful band. To them, the group was a symbol of their homeland. Older Cubans liked having their culture preserved in the sounds of the band. Younger Cubans were grateful for the sense of heritage the band provided. To Cubans of all ages, the MSM was living proof that in a democratic, capitalistic society, anyone could be a success. Miami's Cuban community embraced the band as family and even referred to Gloria as "nuestra Glorita," meaning "our little Gloria."[16]

Actually, Miamians from all ethnic backgrounds were proud of the MSM.[17] Gloria and Emilio Estefan were seen as the band's leaders, and this elevated them to a hero-like status in the city. They were positive role models who did not drink, do drugs, or promote irresponsible sexual behavior. When the MSM was invited to appear on a television show called *Miami Vice*, Gloria said no. The program portrayed Miami as a crime-ridden drug haven, and she would have no part in degrading her hometown. The singer's unwavering loyalty to Miami inspired even more adoration and devotion. The Miami city council renamed the street the Estefans lived on "Miami Sound Machine Boulevard" and presented them with a key to the city.

Most of all, though, Miami loved the couple because they seemed so ordinary. The Estefans had a stable marriage and were attentive to their son. According to one writer, "[Gloria] seemed like the Spanish neighbor next door; this nice woman who had this pleasing voice and wasn't some kind of virtuoso."[18]

However, few women next door are paid a million dollars to sing Pepsi Cola commercials, as Gloria was in 1987.[19] Clearly, Gloria Estefan was no ordinary lady.

CHAPTER SIX

THERE'S SO MUCH IN LIFE THAT'S MEANT FOR YOU

 As the Miami Sound Machine was rising to fame, music videos were becoming a popular form of entertainment. They were also an important advertising tool. Videos combined music, acting, and creative camera work to add a visual dimension to a song. By 1987, it was decided that the MSM needed to make a music video. The thought unnerved Gloria.[1] It didn't help that her video would be competing against those of singers Madonna and Janet Jackson.

In addition to making the video, Epic Records wanted to fine-tune the MSM image. According to

Epic, a band's image is just as important as its music.[2] Image is influenced by many things, including the clothes band members wear, the things they say in public, and the lyrics in their songs. Epic thought it was time to place more emphasis on the band's female vocalist.[3]

Fashion experts were called in to work with Gloria on a wardrobe tailored to compliment her body. Hairdressers and makeup experts made changes, too. Her dark hair was curled into soft ringlets that fell below her shoulders. Even her lipstick shades were changed. In addition, Gloria hired a personal trainer to help her get into better physical condition. At one point, she reported doing six hundred sit-ups and running four miles a day. Before long, the already petite singer weighed in at 102 pounds.

Within months, Gloria had a new look and the band had a new name: Gloria Estefan and the Miami Sound Machine. No longer was the spotlight shared by everyone in the band. Now the focus was on Gloria, with the MSM portrayed as her backup. Gloria was keenly aware of the responsibility that went with this new position. When it came time to make the band's first video, she was so nervous her hands were sweating uncontrollably.[4] In one scene she was to pull a man off a couch, but he slipped out of her grasp. Yet she did not give up. In Gloria's words, "I told myself I was on the line, I had to do this. And do it right."[5]

Not everyone was thrilled with the new focus on Gloria. Kiki Garcia, for example, felt he was being pushed into the background.[6] In his words, "There is no Miami Sound Machine. There is Gloria and Emilio telling a bunch of hired musicians what to do."[7]

Indeed, Kiki and Gloria were the only original MSM members still performing with the band. The Murcianos were gone. Avila had left at the end of 1986 so he could spend more time with his family. Emilio was still the boss, but he did not perform anymore. Instead, he devoted his time to managerial and promotional tasks. He was concentrating then on a new recording, *Let It Loose*, which would be released as a record and a compact disc (CD). The Jerks wrote five songs for the album, three were written by Kiki and Gloria, and Gloria wrote two by herself.

One song, "Anything for You," may have been the song Gloria wrote in the least amount of time ever for her. She penned it while drinking coffee in a hamburger shop, only minutes before she was supposed to record it. Perhaps the spontaneity helped because Gloria sang the song perfectly at the studio the first time through. Everything about the song seemed to be going well until a few days before the recording's final production. Then Gloria decided there was something wrong with the music.[8] So the MSM musicians went back into the studio to work. Seventy-two hours later, the song felt perfect.

Yet after the band's exhaustive work, the producers at Epic did not like "Anything for You" and did not want it on the new album. In response, Emilio Estefan told them the song would be a hit.[9] When *Let It Loose* was released, the last number on it was Gloria's ballad. On May 14, 1988, the song made Miami Sound Machine history by climbing to the top spot on *Billboard*'s pop music chart.[10] Perhaps it was no coincidence that the MSM's first number-one pop song in the United States had been written by Gloria.

Music critics saw the entire *Let It Loose* album as a technical masterpiece. According to one writer, "Sound snaps out of this compact disc like the crack of a whip. Crisp and sharp, with a bite that leaves its mark, the production on the new Miami Sound Machine CD, *Let It Loose*, is about as good as it gets."[11]

As usual, the band planned a tour to promote its latest release. This time, though, Emilio Estefan stayed at home with Nayib, who wanted to play on his Little League baseball team. Gloria would miss them, but she knew the arrangement was best for Nayib. Touring was not a good life for a boy, and he was lonely at home without her or his father.

As the group left Miami, something was different. Now the MSM was really two bands. The Jerks composed one. They created, arranged, and recorded the MSM music. But different musicians went on the road with Gloria. They made up the "second" band, the

Gloria Estefan's new long, soft ringlets soon became her
signature hairstyle.

group the public saw as MSM. There was one thing, though, that never changed: Gloria Estefan was always at center stage and in full command.

Everywhere she went, the five-foot-two-inch dynamo captivated her listeners who joined in the fun. A *Let It Loose* concert was definitely an interactive affair. Amid a sea of raised, clapping hands, audiences sang along with Gloria and managed to dance in packed auditoriums. By the middle of her concerts, Gloria's face was glistening with sweat. She would wipe herself with an MSM emblazoned towel, then wave it over her head and throw it to the crowd. Fans scrambled to catch the star-touched souvenir.

After several rousing dance numbers, the pace would slow and the lights would dim. Then, in her smooth, full voice, Gloria would hold her listeners spellbound with a rendition of "Anything for You." Frequently, audience members held small lighters above their heads as they swayed in time to the music. In the darkened theater, the flickering flames looked like a thousand tiny stars.

From Seattle to Milwaukee to New York City, the band played to one sold-out audience after another. In Las Vegas, a writer noted that there had not been so many people lined up to see a show since Elvis Presley had last appeared there. The MSM also performed to full houses in Madrid, Amsterdam, London, Paris, Stockholm, and Rome.

But fame was not easy. Gloria Estefan once remarked that glamour was something that happened only on stage. Behind the scenes, glamour was nothing more than the product of hard work and a loss of privacy. On the *Let It Loose* tour, for example, the MSM traveled from show to show in a crowded bus outfitted with bunk beds. After a night of performing, exhausted band members fell into their bunks while a driver took them to their next stop. There the band members tumbled out of bed to ready themselves for another night of entertaining.

The MSM seemed to be everywhere—well, almost everywhere. Although its music was popular in Cuba, Gloria still refused to perform in that country. The Cuban government would not have let her, anyway. After all, Gloria's father had once been a part of a plan to topple Castro's regime. Castro had banned MSM music from Cuban radio stations and MSM recordings from stores. But Cubans secretly listened to the band's music and some smuggled MSM records into their homes.

Although Gloria rarely spoke out about her past, she found herself in the middle of a political controversy in 1987. The band had been invited to perform at the Pan American Games in Indianapolis, where Cuban athletes had won many gold medals. These athletes said they would be insulted by an MSM appearance. They threatened to boycott the performance and the band even received death threats.

Gloria felt the whole issue was silly. But she also believed that she had a right to sing wherever she was invited. So she insisted that the band perform. The MSM went on stage as planned, and fortunately, there were no incidents. Gloria later said that by refusing to bow to the Cubans, she was sending the communist government a powerful message. In fact, she felt that the very existence of the MSM showed Castro that he could not wipe out the culture that had existed before he came to power.[12]

But as much as possible, Gloria stayed out of politics. She felt it was a personal subject, and she chose not to share her beliefs with the public. In addition, Gloria knew that speaking out about politics could link her with a cause. This was not what she wanted. Gloria was a singer, and if she was going to be in the public eye, she wanted it to be because of her music.[13]

This did not seem to be a problem. The *Let It Loose* album stayed on the charts for more than two years, and four of its songs became top-ten hits. It would eventually sell more than 4 million copies worldwide.

To Gloria, though, being adored by millions was not the same as being with the people she loved best. Amid the fame and adoration, she missed Emilio and Nayib.[14] Whenever possible, they traveled to see her while she toured. When they were not around, she channeled her loneliness into writing. She also exercised to fend off homesickness. By the time she was halfway through the tour, Gloria was in better physical condition than ever before.

The *Let It Loose* tour ended with two huge concerts in Miami during the fall of 1988. Both were filmed and edited into an award-winning program for cable television. During one part of the concert, Gloria dedicated a new arrangement of "Words Get in the Way" to Julio Iglesias. Iglesias had become a close friend of hers, and he was in the audience that night.

These final concerts represented another kind of end when Kiki announced he was quitting. Then the Jerks left the band, too. According to Galdo, they quit because they were not being given the money or the recognition they deserved. Galdo later reported making several hundred thousand dollars for the *Let It Loose* album while Emilio Estefan made millions.[15]

Of her husband's relationship with other band members, Gloria once reported, "Emilio was always the boss. He was my boss for a year before we even started dating. So even though we have a real democratic system and everyone gets heard, and creatively he's very open minded, business and other decisions are finally going to be made by him."[16]

Yet Galdo believed the Jerks deserved a larger share of the profits and praise. He claimed they were the ones who had created the "Miami Latin" sound for which the band was famous. "That's not the band," he once said, "that's *us*. All you have to do is check out their old albums to hear the difference."[17] But because the Jerks were given little credit for their work, Galdo said that "everybody in the industry thinks that Emilio is the genius behind the whole nine yards."[18]

Few people complained about Gloria, though. Many of the musicians she worked with admired her commitment to perfection.[19] Galdo himself noted that Gloria worked until her music was right, even until four in the morning if that was necessary.

As the Jerks exited, two musicians from the band took their place: Jorge Casas and Clay Ostwald. But changing the band's personnel did not detract from Estefan's fame. At the 1988 American Music Awards, she was named the best international songwriter and the band was named the best pop/rock group. The band also made its way into the *Guinness Book of World Records* that year when 119,000 people danced to "Conga" at a Miami street festival.

Now Gloria wanted a vacation. She and Emilio had recently bought a house on Star Island in Miami's Biscayne Bay. It was a two-story Spanish-style home with a view of the city's skyline. Gloria immediately installed an elevator, though no one in the family needed it. She herself was as fit and trim as ever.

However, in the back of her mind she worried about becoming an invalid as her father had.

For weeks, Gloria relaxed. She went scuba diving and cooked. Although she was on vacation, music was never far from her mind. She learned to play the piano to make songwriting easier and wrote ballads. "Ballads are basically what I'm about," she commented. "I just feel you can express yourself more completely and eloquently in a ballad. It's easier to identify with someone else and form a closer bond with the audience."[20]

By 1989, Gloria had completed another album that included seven songs she had written and arranged. Some of them were sung in English, others in Spanish. Appropriately, this CD was named *Cuts Both Ways*. Perhaps because so much of the music was Gloria Estefan's sole creation, there was no mention of the Miami Sound Machine on the collection. Gloria did not seem to need the group's billing, anyway, because this CD would soon become another success.

Gloria was changing in another way. She was learning that increased fame brought increased requests to speak out on social issues. Some, like an invitation to participate in an antidrug campaign, seemed too important to pass up. Although she still had no desire to be associated with any one issue, Gloria began occasionally promoting a worthy cause.

In early 1990, CBS Records presented her with its prestigious Crystal Globe Award. This award went to musicians whose albums had sold more than 5 million copies outside the United States. This was a rare achievement, and one writer described Gloria's rise to the top as "one of the most underplayed phenomena in the history of non-Anglo music and probably in American pop."[21] Another music critic called Gloria a "veritable one-woman advertisement for the endurance of the American dream."[22]

But no one knew better than Gloria that this level of success was not based on luck. It was the result of constant work, unrelenting desire, and complete dedication. In one song on her new CD Gloria sang, "Get on your feet—get up and take some action!"[23] That, in a nutshell, was Gloria's life.

... AND IT'S
SHINING ON ME

On March 19, 1990, Gloria Maria Estefan stood beside President George Bush to be praised for her part in the campaign to keep kids off drugs. Her photograph had been placed on billboards all over the country with a caption that read, "If you need someone, call a friend. Don't do drugs." Meeting the president of the United States was a memorable experience in Gloria's life. The next day's events would be unforgettable.

In the morning, Gloria, Emilio, Nayib, and three assistants boarded a private tour bus for a five-hour trip. They were headed to Syracuse, New York, where Gloria was scheduled to perform that evening. Not long after the bus started down the highway, Gloria fell asleep on a couch. Nayib studied at the back, and Emilio talked on the phone. When Gloria woke up, the bus was stopped on a highway in Pennsylvania. It was just after noon and snow was falling. An accident ahead had backed up traffic. Later, she would remember how quiet the whole scene was.[1]

Suddenly a truck slammed into the back of the bus with an explosion of noise. The jolt threw Gloria off the sofa like a rag doll. Emilio was flung forward with so much force that he was pulled out of his laced tennis shoes. Just as the bus driver leaned over to help Emilio, the truck accidentally rammed into the bus again, shoving it into a truck in front of them. This tore the side off the bus, narrowly missing the driver. Now snow was falling inside.

Gloria barely noticed. She was worried about Nayib. Emilio had gone to the back of the bus to check on him. He found Nayib on the floor, covered with shoes, bags, and clothes that had fallen from the bunk beds. His shoulder hurt badly, but he seemed all right otherwise. The sight of him gave Gloria courage. Yet she was lying on the floor in excruciating pain. A strange electrical taste in her mouth convinced her she had broken her back. Dread gripped her. All her life Gloria had harbored a secret fear that she would become an invalid.[2] It was this nagging anxiety that had made her put an elevator in her new home. "My God, it's happened," she thought. "The thing that I [have] always feared most."[3]

Other passengers were hurt, too. Later they would learn that Nayib had a broken collarbone, Emilio a broken rib. But at the moment, everyone knew Gloria was injured the most seriously. A passing motorist rushed on board to help. She was a nurse and told Gloria not to move. This was not easy, for the pain was nearly unbearable. Gloria focused her eyes on the ceiling and tried to empty her mind. Nayib held his mother's hand while the others waited for an ambulance. When it finally arrived, the paramedics strapped Gloria onto a stretcher and carried her through a hole in the front of the bus. Emilio watched in fear.

Despite her pain, Gloria could not be given any medication until doctors had examined her. It took almost an hour to get to the nearest hospital, in Scranton, Pennsylvania. There the doctors confirmed the singer's own diagnosis. Gloria had fractured two vertebrae in her back. One doctor reported that if Gloria's spine had moved another half inch after the injury, she would have been permanently paralyzed. Emilio fainted when he heard the news.

Gloria's doctors decided that there were two possible treatments for her injury. First, she could be placed in a body cast for six months while her bones healed.

Despite her busy performing schedule, Gloria makes spending time with her family a priority. This photo of Gloria, with Emilio and Nayib, was taken as they were leaving Miami's airport.

This treatment was safe but offered little hope for a complete recovery. The second course of action was surgery. With surgery, a complicating infection was possible. Furthermore, if something went wrong, Gloria could end up paralyzed for life. But an operation was the only way doctors could see her injury to repair it.

Gloria did not need much time to consider her options. She chose surgery. Emilio immediately started searching for the best doctor for the procedure. He decided on a surgeon in New York City who had performed this operation before. Gloria was put on a hospital helicopter for the flight to New York. Emilio and a doctor were at her side.

Along the way, the helicopter entered some dark clouds and for few moments the sky turned black. When the helicopter passed out of the darkness and into the sunlight, Emilio found himself wishing for the day when Gloria would pass through this terrible darkness in her life.[4] As for the doctor, he was thinking about Gloria's amazing willpower. He later marveled that she hadn't complained of pain during the entire flight. Those who knew Gloria were probably less surprised. Her sister, Becky, had once commented, "[Gloria's] iron, iron on the outside. When something is bothering her, it doesn't show."[5]

Back in Miami, radio stations were playing MSM songs nonstop. Then the city's largest newspaper published a full-page get-well card for Gloria's fans to cut out and mail to her.

On March 22, the star was wheeled into an operating room for a four-hour procedure. The doctor began by making a fourteen-inch incision down the middle of Gloria's back. He then placed an eight-inch steel rod along each side of her spine. The rods would support the broken vertebrae and relieve the pressure on the spinal nerves. Next the doctor scraped chips from one of Gloria's healthy bones and ground them into a powder. He put the powder on the broken vertebrae, where eventually it would grow to the other vertebrae, forming a band of bone around the steel rods. Finally, the doctor sewed the incision shut with more than four hundred stitches. As she lay in the recovery room groggy from anesthesia, Gloria dreamed that she was at the American Music Awards and photographers were calling out her name.

A drawing by Nayib greeted Gloria when she awoke in her private room. It showed her lying on the bus floor with a cartoon bubble above her. Nayib had written one word inside the bubble: "pain."

By evening, television and newspaper reporters were at the hospital to tell a waiting world about Gloria's condition. Fortunately, her doctor could report that the star would regain 95 to 100 percent of her mobility.

During the next two weeks, Gloria stayed at the hospital to begin her long recovery. While there, she received more than fifty thousand get-well cards and four thousand bouquets. Gloria had the flowers distributed to other patients and to people in an AIDS ward at a nearby veterans hospital. She also received calls from many well-wishers, including Elton John, Madonna, Bruce Springsteen, Eric Clapton, Diana Ross, Cyndi Lauper, Whitney Houston, and Celia Cruz. Even President Bush called to see how she was doing.

On April 4, Gloria left New York City on Julio Iglesias's personal jet. She walked off the plane in Miami, leaning on Emilio's arm. Although she was in terrible pain, she smiled and waved to the people who had gathered to welcome her home. She told them that their outpouring of affection had meant more to her than she could ever say.

Back on Star Island, Gloria still faced an uphill battle. For several months, Emilio rose every forty-five minutes during the night to take Gloria for a short walk. Though miserably painful, it was necessary to keep her muscles from stiffening. "She used to walk and cry at the same time," Emilio later remembered.[6]

In addition, three times a week Gloria swam and exercised for six hours straight. Again, the physical therapy was difficult. But hard work had never before stood in the way of Gloria's goals, and it was not going to now. As one friend observed, "Gloria's incredibly disciplined. If they tell her, Gloria, do this, she'll figure out a way to do it three times faster. Her pain just makes her stronger."[7] In August, Gloria told a magazine writer that her current victories were the tiny, everyday things that most people take for granted. For example, putting on her own shoes and washing her face were major accomplishments. Emilio said he lost weight in tears as he watched his wife recover. But Gloria rarely complained. In fact, she reported feeling better and luckier every day.

Gloria did have one worry, however. Her voice doctor had told her that the accident may have affected her singing. Consequently, Gloria did not sing for three months after the crash. She was also experiencing writer's block. Then one day Emilio took her to the recording studio to hear a part of a song he had written. As Gloria listened, the music transformed her fear into inspiration. She finished Emilio's song that very day, delighted to hear her old voice working out the melodies.[8]

The new song, "Coming Out of the Dark," told about Gloria's journey from near-death to wellness. The title phrase had come from Emilio's helicopter experience the day Gloria was flown to New York. The rest of the words were Gloria's. Predictably, the lyrics told that there had been troubles in her life. Just as predictably, though, the words went on to say that there was always an end to *every* despair. In her song, this end was depicted by a shining light.

Now words and music spilled from Gloria. She spent hours in the second-floor studio of her home creating songs. The room was kept bare of furnishings so that she could focus totally on her music. With the guitar she had received on her ninth birthday and an electric keyboard that could play back her tunes, Gloria composed.

As usual, Gloria wrote about what she was feeling and thinking. In one song, she wondered if it was better to face life's challenges or to ignore them. Another song was called "Nayib's Song." In it Gloria wrote, "I'll take care of you and you'll take care of me. It's an ongoing process."[9] A few songs discussed contemporary social problems. For example, one number described sex in the 1990s as dangerous. Making comments about society was something new for Gloria.

In addition to exploring social commentary, Gloria explored different musical styles. When considering whether or not her fans would like this change, Gloria said, "You have to do your music the way you intend it and want it to sound and cross your fingers and hope that people will like it."[10] Before long, Gloria had written enough songs to fill an album.

Next came the work of recording the music. This CD would be the first collection produced in a new state-of-the art recording studio owned by the Estefans.

The collection would be called *Into the Light* to symbolize Gloria's victory over her ordeal.

Of course, with an upcoming album, plans for a tour could not be far off. As various business arrangements were made and songs were rehearsed, Emilio hired a choreographer named Kenny Ortega to create dances for the show. Gradually, Gloria's workouts changed from physical therapy to grueling rehearsals for complicated dance numbers.

Gloria also tended to the many other details connected with an upcoming tour. There were costumes to try on, photo sessions for publicity, and decisions regarding souvenir memorabilia. There were two videos to rehearse for and to film. Of her never-ending energy, Ortega once commented, "The highlight of working with Gloria has always been that she is one of the most focused and determined people to work with."[11] In many ways, the just-mended Gloria seemed like the Gloria of old.

But the accident had changed her. For months after the wreck, she felt nervous riding in a car.[12] Characteristically, though, Gloria faced her fear and climbed into vehicles as needed. There was one difference, however: She always wore a seat belt.

In addition, Gloria emerged from her experience with a new appreciation for life. "It's very hard to stress me out now. It's hard to get me in an uproar about anything because most things have little significance compared with what I almost lost."[13] She added, "I would not recommend a brush with death to anybody, but if you are going to have it, at least get some good stuff out of it."[14]

Day by day, Gloria grew stronger. As usual, she set her personal goals high. She was not content with returning to the stage as the same entertainer she was before the accident. Gloria meant to be better.[15] Her doctors seemed to think this was impossible. They were pleased with her recovery and said she could do everything but sky dive, play football, and do back flips.

Sometimes Gloria joked, too. "How do you pick up Gloria Estefan?" she would ask. "With a magnet!" came her quick reply. Emilio was awed by his wife's recovery, and he sometimes referred to her as "robo-cop." Perhaps he should have called her "robo-singer," though, for Gloria Estefan was about to make a remarkable comeback!

CHAPTER EIGHT

EVERLASTING GLORIA

 It was March 1, 1991, and Gloria Estefan was standing backstage at the Miami Arena, wearing a tight-fitting blue jumpsuit with a matching headpiece. Her heart was pounding. In just a few moments she would be performing her first concert since the bus accident almost one year earlier, a performance Estefan later called the most emotional premiere of her career.[1]

Soon it was showtime, and Estefan was leaping through a curtain of ribbons with four other dancers. After a few twists and turns about the stage, Estefan removed her headpiece to reveal her identity. The audience erupted in a roar of adoration. Suddenly, all of Estefan's work, sweat, and hours of pain became worth it. She was back onstage singing the music she loved.

Estefan's new show was called *Into the Light*. It featured her "victory" song, "Coming Out of the Dark." The number had been expertly arranged and choreographed to make it a showcase emphasizing Estefan's recovery. A gospel chorus sang the backup parts and gave the song an air of spirituality.

After Gloria performed a few old favorites for the hometown crowd, she paused to thank her fans. "So many people got behind me and gave me a reason to want to come back fast and made me feel strong. Knowing how caring people can be, how much they gave me—that has changed me forever."[2]

Next, Gloria worked her way through a medley of ballads at the front of the stage. There, security guards allowed a dozen or so fans to approach her for a handshake or a hug. Most brought her a long-stemmed red rose. Some handed her a note or a stuffed animal. A few whispered a personal message into her ear while she sang.

Watching Gloria perform made one believe she had never been gone. Her voice was clear, her dance routines exact, and her performance style top-notch.

By the concert's end, the critics all seemed to agree—Gloria was most definitely back![3]

Audiences packed auditoriums all across the country to witness for themselves Gloria's remarkable recovery. Then, exactly one year after Gloria's accident, "Coming Out of the Dark" hit the number-one spot on the pop music chart.

In addition to her U.S. success, Gloria remained an international sensation. In England, more than one hundred fifty thousand fans came to her latest show, using the tickets they had saved from her last tour. They may have had the longest wait in history for a concert. Fans in the Netherlands were patient, too. They stood for hours in freezing weather to buy tickets because, as one man put it, "Gloria Estefan's worth it."[4] By the tour's end, Gloria had traveled to nine countries on five continents and sung to more than 5 million people.

In May, Gloria went to Las Vegas to receive a lifetime achievement award from an organization called Premio Lo Nuestro a la Musica Latina. It was the Latin American equivalent of a Grammy Award.

Back at home, Gloria worked on an album of her old hits. Then all work ceased in September 1992 when Hurricane Andrew struck southern Florida. Its winds raged at 160 miles an hour, destroying everything in its path. Cars were flattened, homes were ripped apart, and trees were pulled up by their roots.

Estefan received an award in 1991 for her contribution to Latin American music.

In the words of one Floridian, "You haven't lived through anything until you find a trailer flying into your house. There are no words to describe the fear."[5]

As for the Estefans, they waited out the storm inside their recording studio. When the winds finally calmed, they emerged to find their house in one piece. Other families were less fortunate. Hundreds of Florida residents now faced a future without jobs, homes, or families.

Gloria took prompt action. "I owe these people so much," she explained." After all, they were there for me when I had the accident. They went out to their churches and synagogues and prayed for me. They didn't even know me personally."[6] So she and Emilio organized a benefit concert for victims of the hurricane. On September 26, Whoopi Goldberg, Paul Simon, Rosie O'Donnell, and several other celebrities entertained fifty-five thousand people at Miami's Joe Robbie Stadium. Their marathon show raised almost $2 million for the hurricane fund.

For Gloria, however, this was not enough. So she recorded a new ballad and donated all of its profits to Andrew's victims. The song was called "Always Tomorrow," and it expressed Gloria's beliefs about handling tragedy. "You can sit there and wallow," she said. "You weep for what's gone and then you move ahead."[7]

Gloria's good works were not going unnoticed. In 1992, she was showered with honors for her charitable endeavors. The B'nai B'rith Society, the oldest and largest Jewish service organization, named Gloria the Humanitarian of the Year. Then came a special honor when President Bush chose her to be a public delegate and working member of the United Nations.

Estefan began 1993 by cohosting the 20th Annual American Music Awards in Los Angeles. That same year she would receive a star with her name on it on Hollywood's legendary Walk of Fame. In addition, Estefan was given the Ellis Island Medal of Honor, the Hispanic Heritage Award, an honorary doctorate degree from the University of Miami, and recognition from the Alexis de Tocqueville Society for her outstanding philanthropy. Of this never-ending flow of praise, Gloria said that she was just a normal person who liked to do good things. In Miami, people treated her like a saint.[8]

Gloria loved Miami right back. This mutual admiration made the singer a bridge between the city's Latin American population and those of the mainstream culture. Actually, Gloria's appeal helped close this cultural gap across the United States.

Yet Gloria Maria Fajardo Estefan never forgot her roots. She once summed up her feelings about her heritage by saying, "I don't feel Cuban or American. I guess I feel 'Latin Miami.'"[9] In June 1993, she released

The CD was called *Hold Me, Thrill Me, Kiss Me* after a song originally made popular by Mel Carter. Because all of the songs on the CD were classics, Estefan felt it would not need the promotion of a tour. This would allow her to stay home and rest—just as soon as she completed a new music video.

Although she was five months into her pregnancy, Estefan stood on the roof of a Miami skyscraper one clear night to shoot a video for the song "Turn the Beat Around." Departing from her signature curls, Estefan's hair was pulled tightly back and gathered at the nape of her neck. The hairdo accentuated her face with its flawless complexion, long nose, and lively eyes. The camera panned Gloria carefully in shots that didn't show her pregnancy. As she sang, a helicopter flew in and out of the video to create an interesting audio addition to the music. The background was a spectacular view of Miami's skyscrapers and night lights.

Then when Gloria was nine months pregnant, another video was made for her latest CD. Gloria didn't participate in the filming of this one though. Instead, five look-alikes were chosen to act in it. Four of them were actually men! The actors were outfitted in the various costumes Gloria had worn in previous videos. They paraded around on stage, mouthing the words to Gloria's song "Everlasting Love" while the camera caught them in dizzying shots. Later, clips of Gloria from old videos were woven into this video. The result

Gloria and Emilio with their new daughter, Emily Marie, in March 1995.

was a kind of puzzle to viewers, who tried to identify the real Gloria among the stand-ins.

As this new video was finding its way into America's homes, Gloria was being pushed into a hospital delivery room. Doctors needed to perform a cesarean birth, and Emilio had to be coaxed into attending. According to Gloria, he did well until someone announced that the baby was coming. At that point, he turned green and had to sit down. The sight of his infant daughter revived him, though. She was named Emily Marie, and her godfather was the famous musician Quincy Jones. Emilio later reported that little Emily would definitely be spoiled.

But Gloria did not hire a nanny to take care of Emily. Instead, she basked in the glory of changing diapers and cooing at her daughter. She had more time to spend with Nayib, too, who was becoming something of a musician himself. He was active in his school band and enjoyed playing the drums when he was at home. Nayib also practiced magic, hoping to work out a professional act of his own.

While her family grew up around her, Gloria continued to make music. Her next project was a CD of original songs sung in Spanish. It would be called *Abriendo Puertas* ("Opening Doors"). Its very title was a reminder that for Gloria, music was a powerful form of communication.

LIFE IN THE
NOT-SO-FAST LANE

 Gloria Estefan likes to start her day with a cup of Cuban coffee served to her in bed. While she sips the strong brew, her housekeeper opens the bedroom shutters to reveal a breathtaking view of the ocean. Once Estefan is up, she has breakfast, then exercises before going to work.

As he has for many years, Emilio handles the family's business, a corporation called Estefan Enterprises. Emilio built this company from scratch. It produces all of Estefan's albums, as well as the music of other artists. Estefan Enterprises also owns hotels, restaurants, and resorts along Miami's famous beaches. In addition, Emilio manages his wife's career. As her closest adviser, he has been criticized as being too controlling of his wife's professional life. To these comments, Emilio says that Gloria makes her own decisions. "If she is offered ten million dollars to do a commercial and she doesn't want to do it, that's the end of it. Because I have to respect that she's a very smart woman."[1]

One thing is definite. Emilio no longer tells Gloria that she could improve herself by 95 percent. Gone, too, are the days when Gloria studies a videotape of each of her performances. "I was already there," she said. "It's like working again, like reliving the whole experience. I let Emilio watch it."[2]

Emilio also takes care of running the house. This frees Gloria to be with her children. She knows how precious time with them is, once lamenting that when Nayib was young, she missed too many baseball games. But now her family is the center of her life, and she reserves the typical "mothering" tasks for herself. "I don't spank my kids," she once reported. "I punish."[3] One of her favorite disciplining methods for Nayib is to make him write sentences over and over again. Gloria recalls the incident that resulted in Nayib's having to pen "I will not moon the tour boats that pass by."[4] Nayib has gotten himself into more serious trouble, too. He was once expelled from his exclusive private school for calling a friend's mother and pretending to be a school official. Nayib told the mother that her son had been suspended for throwing food in the cafeteria. And tabloid newspapers once reported that Nayib was engaged to a thirty-nine-year-old woman. While Estefan denied their engagement, she acknowledged that her son did like older women. As for the Estefans, their marriage seems to be as strong as ever.

Because Estefan hates to shop for clothes, Emilio usually buys them for her. In fact, other than her performances, she likes to stay at home. Occasionally, she does go out to her favorite Cuban restaurant, located in a Miami shopping mall. But there are no maitre d's there. The restaurant is a typical diner with formica tables and waitresses wearing pastel uniforms.

In the late summer of 1995, Estefan traveled to the United States naval base at Guantanamo Bay, Cuba. There, she sang a concert for the troops and the fifteen thousand Cubans living on the base who were waiting for permission to move to the United States. Many had made banners proclaiming "We Love You, Gloria." As she got ready for the concert, Estefan thought about her father. Then, it was showtime, and Estefan was onstage. Amplifiers blasted the music loud enough to be heard across the border of the base, where Cuban territory begins. Estefan sang "Conga" and "Abriendo Puertas." As an encore, she chose "Mi Tierra," her own song that calls Cuba her homeland that suffers, and her eyes glistened with tears.

Estefan and one of her dalmations promote water safety.

Then, it was time to return to Miami. Back on Star Island, Estefan is content to stay at home. It's no wonder. The Estefans' house is more like a resort than a residence. The yard is landscaped with palm trees, exotic flowers, and a waterfall. In the backyard is a swimming pool. Five dalmatians and three wallabies romp the grounds (yes, wallabies!).

In 1995, Estefan and Emilio built a second house behind their five-bedroom home, then connected the two with a covered walkway. The new house includes a small movie theater and a room just for the dogs. The Estefan home is lived-in but elegant. Emily's toys are scattered amid comfortable furnishings and priceless pieces of Latin American art.

Just outside the Estefans' door is a private dock. Motorboating has become one of Estefan's favorite hobbies. Unfortunately, her passion was marred by tragedy one September afternoon in 1995. That day, the Estefans had hopped aboard their thirty-foot boat for a short cruise. As Emilio drove it slowly through crowded waters, a man on a waterbike appeared out of nowhere. He sped up to the boat and tried to jump on its wake. When he lost his balance, his bike slammed into the side of the Estefan boat. Both he and his passenger were thrown off the bike. The passenger landed in open water, but the driver was sucked under the boat and into its propellers.[5]

Emilio immediately jumped into the shark-infested water to help the man. While he struggled to get him on board, Estefan called 911 for help. Other boaters arriving on the scene helped get the two to shore where paramedics were waiting. The bike passenger suffered cuts and bruises, but was not seriously hurt. Tragically, the driver could not be saved; he died before reaching the hospital.[6]

A police investigation concluded that the Estefans were not at fault. In fact, it reported, the couple had done everything possible to save the young man. Even though she was not to blame, the experience devastated Estefan. For a while, she was too distraught to speak about the accident.[7] She did, however, call the man's family to express her sympathy.

Little by little, Estefan's life returned to normal. She continued to work on her music, and in 1996 a new CD called *Destiny* was released. It included a song written for the 1996 Olympics: "Reach." Then came another world tour, the first since Emily's birth. It opened with an act by a new magician—Nayib Estefan.

Estefan still devotes a large portion of her time to humanitarian efforts. For example, she is involved in AIDS education and water-safety programs. Gloria hopes that her fame will make people pay attention to her message.

At this 1996 rally, Emilio, Gloria, and Mrs. Fajardo voice their support for a Cuban refugee rescue operation called Brothers to the Rescue.

Yet the singer is still guarded about her personal life, and some critics have suggested that this private side may be a crucial factor in Estefan's success.[8] They believe that because the star isn't always talking about her feelings, those feelings come through in her lyrics and her songs. As one writer asks, is it "because she has chosen not to sell her soul to the front page that her voice actually expresses so [much emotion]?"[9] Indeed, it is the emotion communicated through Estefan's

107

In April 1996 Estefan was honored by VH1. During the program she performed the song she had written for the 1996 Olympics, "Reach."

songs that draw so many people to her music. Many fans even seem to feel like a personal friend of the star's. Estefan herself once said, "Singing is the closest thing [to knowing] someone."[10]

The once-shy young woman has blossomed into a superstar who is sure of her beauty and her talent without being arrogant. Her soft auburn hair is cut in a style that frames her uniquely beautiful face. Onstage, Estefan is as talented as ever. Time has mellowed some of the exuberance of her younger years, yet her act is still vibrant.

Estefan's creativity shows no sign of slowing, either, and she intends to keep making music. It is, after all, what she has always been about. But because she wants to concentrate on music, the star won't do any more commercials or promote products such as Gloria Estefan dolls. The singer's fame and fortune aren't likely to suffer from this decision. Estefan already has fifty platinum albums to her name, and millions of fans around the world eagerly purchase each new CD she records. Furthermore, the family business, Estefan Enterprises, is estimated to be worth $40 million.[11]

But life's tragedies have taught Estefan to count her blessings rather than her wealth. Among them are the man who has stood beside her for more than twenty years, two beautiful children, and a life free of financial worry. So why does Gloria Estefan keep working? Simple. Because she loves to sing.

CHRONOLOGY

1957—Gloria Maria Fajardo is born in Havana, Cuba, on September 1.

1958—The Fajardo family flees Fidel Castro's communist regime and moves to Miami, Florida.

1961—Gloria's father, José Fajardo, is captured by the Cuban government during the Bay of Pigs invasion.

1962—José Fajardo returns to the United States and joins the army.

1966—Fajardo is sent to Vietnam. Gloria receives a guitar for her birthday. She takes guitar lessons and enjoys learning songs on her own.

1968—Fajardo returns from Vietnam very ill. Gloria takes care of him while her mother works and attends night school. Whenever she has time, Gloria listens to the radio and sings.

1975—Gloria graduates from high school, starts college, and joins Emilio Estefan's band, the Miami Latin Boys. The band is renamed the Miami Sound Machine. Its members are Gloria, her cousin Merci Fajardo, Emilio Estefan, Juan Avila, Enrique Garcia, and Raul Murciano.

1978—Gloria graduates from the University of Miami and marries Estefan on her birthday. The Miami Sound Machine (MSM) releases two albums for a local record company.

1980—Gloria Estefan's father dies and her first child, Nayib, is born. The MSM obtains a recording contract with Discos CBS International.

1980 –1983—The MSM records four albums of pop music in Spanish and makes tours to Latin America. The group gains immense popularity there, selling millions of records and drawing huge concert audiences. As of yet, though, the group is relatively unknown in the United States. Murciano and Merci Fajardo marry. They leave the group in 1982.

1984— MSM drummer, Kiki Garcia, writes "Dr. Beat." The song hits the U.S. pop charts, bringing the MSM closer to crossing over into the U.S. market. The band records its first all-English album, *Eyes of Innocence.*

1985—A new single, "Conga," makes recording history when it appears on four different pop charts at once. Three new musicians who call themselves "The Jerks" are hired to work with the band. The band's second English album, *Primitive Love*, is released, and it produces two more top-ten hits.

1986— The MSM gains wide recognition and popularity in the U.S. pop market. Band members are named Best New Pop Artists and Top Pop Singles Artists at the American Music Awards. Juan Avila resigns from the band.

1987—The MSM produces its first music video. The band is renamed Gloria Estefan and the Miami Sound Machine upon the release of a new album *Let It Loose*. Emilio stops performing with the group.

1988—Estefan's ballad "Anything for You" becomes the MSM's first number-one pop hit. At the American Music Awards, Estefan is named Songwriter of the Year, and the band is named Best Pop/Rock Group of the Year. Kiki Garcia and the Three Jerks leave the band.

1989— By now, Estefan is the only original member left. When *Cuts Both Ways* is released, there is no mention of the MSM on its cover.

1990—Estefan's back is broken in a bus accident. She spends the next year recovering, writing music, and preparing for her stage comeback.

1991—In March, Estefan launches a successful comeback tour called *Into the Light*. Its feature song, "Coming out of the Dark," reaches number one on the pop charts.

1992—After Hurricane Andrew hits Florida, Estefan raises thousands of dollars to aid its victims.

1994— Estefan's second child, Emily, is born.

1995—Estefan performs a concert at the U.S. Guantanamo naval base in Cuba. Later that year, a waterbike rams into the Estefan's motorboat, killing the driver of the bike.

1996— After a five-year sabbatical, Estefan embarks on another world tour. She also co-writes the unofficial theme song for the 1996 Olympics and performs it at the closing ceremonies in Atlanta, Georgia.

SELECTED DISCOGRAPHY

Albums, Compact Discs, and Hit Singles

Renacer (1978)

Miami Sound Machine (1978)

MSM Imported (1979)

MSM (1980)

Otra Vez (1981)

Rio (1982)

A Toda Maquina (1984)

Primitive Love (1985)
"Words Get in the Way"
"Bad Boy"—Gold Record
"Conga"—Gold Record

Let It Loose (1987)
"Anything for You"—Gold Record
"1-2-3"
"Rhythm Is Gonna Get You"
"Can't Stay Away from You"

Cuts Both Ways (1989)
  "Don't Wanna Lose You"—Gold Record
  "Here We Are"

Into the Light (1991)
  "Coming Out of the Dark"

Greatest Hits (1992)

Mi Tierra (1993)
  —Grammy Award

Christmas Through Your Eyes (1993)

Hold Me, Thrill Me, Kiss Me (1994)
  "Everlasting Love"

Abriendo Puertas (1995)
  —Grammy Award

Destiny (1996)

VIDEOS

Homecoming Concert, produced by Paul Flattery (New York: CBS Music Video Enterprises, CBS Records, 1989).

Evolution, produced by Emilio Estefan, Jr. (New York: CBS Music Video Enterprises, CBS Records, 1990).

Coming Out of the Dark, produced by Emilio Estefan, Jr. (New York: Sony Music Video Enterprises, Sony Music Entertainment, 1991).

Into the Light, produced by Emilio Estefan, Jr. (New York: Sony Music Video Enterprises, Sony Music Entertainment, 1992).

CHAPTER NOTES

CHAPTER 1. LIKE AN ANGEL GONE AWOL

1. James Brady, "In Step with Gloria Estefan," *Parade Magazine*, April 28, 1996, p. 18.

2. "Ole! Gloria Estefan," *New York Times Magazine*, October 23, 1994, p. 35.

CHAPTER 2. I'LL TAKE CARE OF YOU

1. Louis A. Perez, Jr., *Cuba: Between Reform and Revolution* (New York: Oxford University Press, 1995), p. 30.

2. Ibid., p. 13.

3. Argentina Palacios, *Standing Tall: The Stories of Ten Hispanic Americans* (New York: Scholastic, Inc., 1994), pp. 194–195.

4. Margaret Rooke and Ruby Millington, "Gloria Estefan," *Telegraph Magazine*, October 22, 1994.

5. C. K. Yearly, "Cubans in Miami," *Commonweal*, November 19, 1965, p. 211.

6. Rebecca Stefoff, *Gloria Estefan* (New York: Chelsea House, 1991), p. 35.

7. Palacios, p. 198.

8. *Current Biography*, October 1995, p. 148.

9. Biographical/promotional material from Estefan Enterprises, 1995.

10. Rooke and Millington.

11. Video Hits One, television special, "Motherload: Gloria Estefan" (1996).

12. Diane Telgen and Jim Kamp, eds., *Notable Hispanic American Women* (Detroit: Gale Research Inc., 1993), p. 149.

13. Kathryn Casey, "My Miracle," *Ladies Home Journal*, August 1990, p. 152.

14. Richard Harrington, "Miami Voice," *Washington Post*, July 17, 1988, p. G4.

15. Telgen and Kamp, p. 149.
16. *Current Biography*, p. 148.
17. "Ole! Gloria Estefan," p. 34.

CHAPTER 3. WHAT A DIFFERENCE A DAY MAKES

1. "Ole! Gloria Estefan," *New York Times Magazine*, October 23, 1994, p. 34.

2. *Current Biography*, October 1995, p. 19.

3. Biographical/promotional material from Estefan Enterprises, 1995.

4. Rebecca Stefoff, *Gloria Estefan* (New York: Chelsea House, 1991), p. 50.

5. Argentina Palacios, *Standing Tall: The Stories of Ten Hispanic Americans* (New York: Scholastic, Inc., 1994), p. 202.

6. Stefoff, p. 52.

7. Steve Dougherty, "One Step at a Time," *People Weekly*, June 25, 1990, p. 82.

8. George Flowers and Jesse Nash, "Gloria Estefan," *Seventeen*, December 1989, p. 70.

9. Stefoff, p. 57.

10. Ibid., p. 55.

11. David Wild, "Sweet Inspirations," *Rolling Stone*, September 21, 1989, p. 69.

12. Grace Catalano, *Gloria Estefan* (New York: St. Martin's Press, 1991), p. 48.

CHAPTER 4. BORN TO SING

1. Margaret Rooke and Ruby Millington, "Gloria Estefan," *Telegraph Magazine*, October 22, 1994.

2. Rebecca Stefoff, *Gloria Estefan* (New York: Chelsea House, 1991), p. 60.

3. Ibid., p. 64.

4. Richard Harrington, "Miami Voice," *Washington Post*, July 17, 1988, p. G5.

5. Ibid.

6. Michael L. LaBlanc, ed., *Contemporary Musicians* (Detroit: Gale Research Inc., 1990) pp. 70–71.

7. Ibid., p. 71.

8. Rooke and Millington.

9. Harrington, p. G5.

10. Daisann McLane, "The Power and the Gloria." *Rolling Stone*, June 14, 1990, p. 80.

11. Ibid.

CHAPTER 5. BREAKTHROUGH!

1. Grace Catalano, *Gloria Estefan* (New York: St. Martin's Press, 1991), pp. 65–66.

2. Ibid.

3. Ibid., p. 72.

4. Diane Telgen and Jim Kamp, eds., *Notable Hispanic American Women* (Detroit: Gale Research Inc., 1993), p. 150.

5. Daisann McLane, "The Power and the Gloria," *Rolling Stone*, June 14, 1990, p. 80.

6. Richard Harrington, "Miami Voice," *Washington Post*, July 17, 1988, p. G5.

7. Catalano, p. 63.

8. George Flowers and Jesse Nash, "Gloria Estefan," *Seventeen*, December 1989, p. 70.

9. "Conga," words and music by Enrique E. Garcia (Foreign Imported Productions and Publishing, [BMI]).

10. Catalano, p. 82.

11. *Current Biography*, October 1995, p. 150.

12. Margaret Rooke and Ruby Millington, "Gloria Estefan," *Telegraph Magazine*, October 22, 1994.

13. Linda Marx, "Throw the Switch on the Miami Sound Machine, and Pop Go the Hit Singles," *People Weekly*, October 27, 1986, p. 78.

14. Cyn Zarco, "Gloria Estefan Stops the Music," *USA Weekend*, April 3, 1994, p. 10.

15. Harrington, p. G5.

16. *Current Biography*, October 1995, p. 157.

17. Ibid., p. 147.

18. Laura Morice, "Gloria Hallelujah!" *McCall's*, July 1995, p. 72.

19. Marx, p. 78.

CHAPTER 6. THERE'S SO MUCH IN LIFE THAT'S MEANT FOR YOU

1. Richard Harrington, "Miami Voice," *Washington Post*, July 17, 1998, p. G5.

2. Grace Catalano, *Gloria Estefan* (New York: St. Martin's Press, 1991), p. 91.

3. Michael L. LaBlanc, ed., *Contemporary Musicians* (Detroit: Gale Research Inc., 1990), p. 71.

4. Harrington, p. G5.

5. Ibid.

6. Daisann McLane, "The Power and the Gloria," *Rolling Stone*, June 14, 1990, p. 80.

7. Rebecca Stefoff, *Gloria Estefan* (New York: Chelsea House, 1991), p. 85.

8. Catalano, p. 94.

9. Ibid., p. 95.

10. Joel Whitburn, *Pop Singles Annual: 1955–1990* (Menominee Falls, Wis.: Record Research, 1991), p. 527.

11. Catalano, p. 150.

12. Harrington, p. G5.

13. Ibid.

14. Laura Morice, "Gloria Hallelujah!" *McCall's*, July 1995, p. 73.

15. McLane, p. 80.

16. Harrington, p. G5.

17. McLane, p. 80.

18. Ibid.

19. Ibid.

20. Diane Telgen and Jim Kamp, eds., *Notable Hispanic American Women* (Detroit: Gale Research Inc., 1993), p. 150.

21. "Ole! Gloria Estefan," *New York Times Magazine*, October 23, 1994, p. 34.

22. *Current Biography*, October 1995, p. 157.

23. From "Get on Your Feet," words and music by John DeFaria, Jorge Casas, and Clay Ostwald (Foreign Imported Productions and Publications [BMI]/Estefan Music, Publishing, 1988).

CHAPTER 7. . . . AND IT'S SHINING ON ME

1. Kathryn Casey, "My Miracle," *Ladies Home Journal*, August 1990, p. 100.
2. Ibid., p. 152.
3. Ibid.
4. Emilio Estefan, Jr., *exec.* producer, "Coming Out of the Dark" video (New York: Sony Music Video Enterprises, l991).
5. Daisann McLane, "The Power and the Gloria," *Rolling Stone*, June 14, 1990, p. 80.
6. Laura Morice, "Gloria Hallelujah!" *McCall's*, July 1995, p. 72.
7. McLane, p. 80.
8. Steve Dougherty, "A Year after Her Brush with Disaster, Gloria Estefan Dances out of the Dark with a New Album and World Tour," *People Weekly*, February 18, 1991, p. 118.
9. "Nayib's Song," (Sony Music Entertainment, 1991).
10. Emilio Estefan, Jr., *exec.* producer, "Coming Out of the Dark" video (New York: Sony Music Video Enterprises, 1991).
11. Ibid.
12. Casey, p. 155.
13. Dougherty, p. 118.
14. "Ole! Gloria Estefan," *New York Times Magazine*, October 23, 1994, p. 34.
15. Steve Dougherty, "One Step at a Time," *People Weekly*, June 25, 1990, p. 82.

CHAPTER 8. EVERLASTING GLORIA

1. Emilio Estefan, Jr., *exec.* producer, "Coming Out of the Dark" video (New York: Sony Music Video Enterprises, 1991).
2. Steve Dougherty, "A Year after Her Brush with Disaster, Gloria Estefan Dances out of the Dark with a New Album and World Tour," *People Weekly*, February 18, 1991, p. 118.
3. John Lannert, "'Talent in Action: Gloria Estefan," *Billboard*, March 23, 1991, p. 35.
4. Emilio Estefan, Jr., "Coming Out of the Dark" video.
5. "What Went Wrong," *Newsweek*, September 7, 1992, p. 23.
6. Argentina Palacios, *Standing Tall: The Stories of Ten Hispanic Americans* (New York: Scholastic Inc., 1994), p. 215.

7. Pam Lambert and Cindy Dampier, "Miami Spells Hurricane Relief G-L-O-R-I-A," *People Weekly*, October 12, 1992, p. 47.

8. Cyn Zarco, "Gloria Estefan Stops the Music," *USA Weekend*, April 3, 1994, p. 10.

9. Jay Cocks, "Dancing on the Charts," *Time*, May 28, 1990, p. 87.

10. "Ole! Gloria Estefan," *New York Times Magazine*, October 23, 1994, p. 35.

CHAPTER 9. LIFE IN THE NOT-SO-FAST LANE

1. Laura Morice, "Gloria Hallelujah!" *McCall's*, July 1995, p. 72.

2. Cyn Zarco, "Gloria Estefan Stops the Music," *USA Weekend*, April 3, 1994, p. 10.

3. Peter Castro, "Talking with . . . Gloria Estefan," *People Weekly*, November 6, 1995, p. 27.

4. Ibid.

5. David Hancock and Rick Jervis, "Man Killed as Sea Craft Hits Estefans," *Miami Herald*, September 25, 1995, p. 7A.

6. Peter Castro, Cindy Dampier, and Mary Esselman, "Water Hazard," *People Weekly*, October 9, 1995, p. 66.

7. Ibid.

8. "Ole! Gloria Estefan," *New York Times Magazine*, October 23, 1984, p. 34.

9. Ibid.

10. Emilio Estefan, Jr., exec. producer, "Coming Out of the Dark" video (New York: Sony Music Video Enterprises, 1991).

11. Zarco, p. 10.

FURTHER READING

Catalano, Grace. *Gloria Estefan*. New York: St. Martin's Press, 1991.

Giacobello, John. *Choosing a Career in Music*. New York: Rosen Publishing Group, 1996.

Novas, Himilce. *The Hispanic 100*. New York: Carol Publishing Group, 1995.

Palacios, Argentina. *Standing Tall: The Stories of Ten Hispanic Americans*. New York: Scholastic, 1994.

Rodriguez, Janel. *Gloria Estefan*. Chatham, N.J.: Raintree Steck-Vaughn, 1996.

Steffof, Rebecca. *Gloria Estefan*. New York: Chelsea House, 1991.

INDEX